Bad to the Bone
NASTIEST ANIMALS

Honey Badgers

By Marie Roesser

Gareth Stevens
PUBLISHING

Please visit our website, www.garethstevens.com. For a free color catalog of all our high-quality books, call toll free 1-800-542-2595 or fax 1-877-542-2596.

Library of Congress Cataloging-in-Publication Data

Roesser, Marie, author.
 Honey badgers / Marie Roesser.
     pages cm. — (Bad to the bone. Nastiest animals)
 Includes bibliographical references and index.
 ISBN 978-1-4824-1954-2 (pbk.)
 ISBN 978-1-4824-1953-5 (6 pack)
 ISBN 978-1-4824-1955-9 (library binding)
 1. Honey badger—Juvenile literature. I. Title.
 QL737.C25R645 2015
 599.76'62—dc23

                                2014020524

First Edition

Published in 2015 by
Gareth Stevens Publishing
111 East 14th Street, Suite 349
New York, NY 10003

Copyright © 2015 Gareth Stevens Publishing

Designer: Michael Flynn
Editor: Therese Shea

Photo credits: Cover, p. 1 Erwin Niemand/Shutterstock.com; cover, pp. 1–24 (series art) foxie/Shutterstock.com; cover, pp. 1–24 (series art) Larysa Ray/Shutterstock.com; cover, pp. 1–24 (series art) LeksusTuss/Shutterstock.com; p. 5 Camptoloma/Shutterstock.com; p. 7 Kobie Douglas/Shutterstock.com; p. 9 (honey badger) Mary Ann McDonald/ Visuals Unlimited, Inc./Getty Images; p. 9 (map) ekler/Shutterstock.com; p. 11 Christian Heinrich/Getty Images; p. 13 Suzi Eszterhas/Minden Pictures/Getty Images; pp. 15, 17 Michal Cizek/Stringer/AFP/Getty Images; p. 19 (skunk) Geoffrey Kuchera/Shutterstock.com; p. 19 (honey badger) Ewan Chesser/Shutterstock.com; p. 21 Totodu74/Wikipedia.com.

Printed in the United States of America

CPSIA compliance information: Batch #CW15GS: For further information contact Gareth Stevens, New York, New York at 1-800-542-2595.

Contents

Words in the glossary appear in **bold** type the first time they are used in the text.

Not So Cute

The name "honey badger" sounds cute. You might picture a cuddly, furry animal that likes to eat honey. However, if you'd ever seen a honey badger fight, you wouldn't want to cuddle it!

Honey badgers are known as some of the meanest animals on Earth. They have no problem taking on larger animals—even lions. Why would a furry little animal fight the king of the beasts? It's not that honey badgers aren't smart. They're incredibly tough!

That's Nasty!

The honey badger is called the "most fearless animal in the world" in the Guinness Book of World Records.

The honey badger is also called a ratel.

One Bad Weasel

Badgers are a kind of **weasel**. Badgers have a flat, furry body and short legs with long claws.

Honey badgers are mostly black. However, they have a grayish-white stripe that runs from the top of their head to their tail. They're often 2.5 feet to 3 feet (76 to 91 cm) long and up to 12 inches (30 cm) tall at the shoulder. That may not seem so big, but honey badgers have **adaptations** that make them fearsome fighters.

Honey badgers may weigh up to 30 pounds (13.6 kg).

Not in Your Backyard

Most of us don't get to see honey badgers in their **habitat**. They live in Africa, the Middle East, Central Asia, and India. They make their homes in grasslands, forests, and mountains. They don't like places that are too hot like deserts or too wet like rainforests.

Honey badgers use their long claws to dig **burrows** to live in. They're mostly nocturnal, which means they come out at night to look for something to eat. What do they like to eat? They're not picky. They eat almost anything!

That's Nasty!

Honey badgers find more than half the things they eat while digging underground.

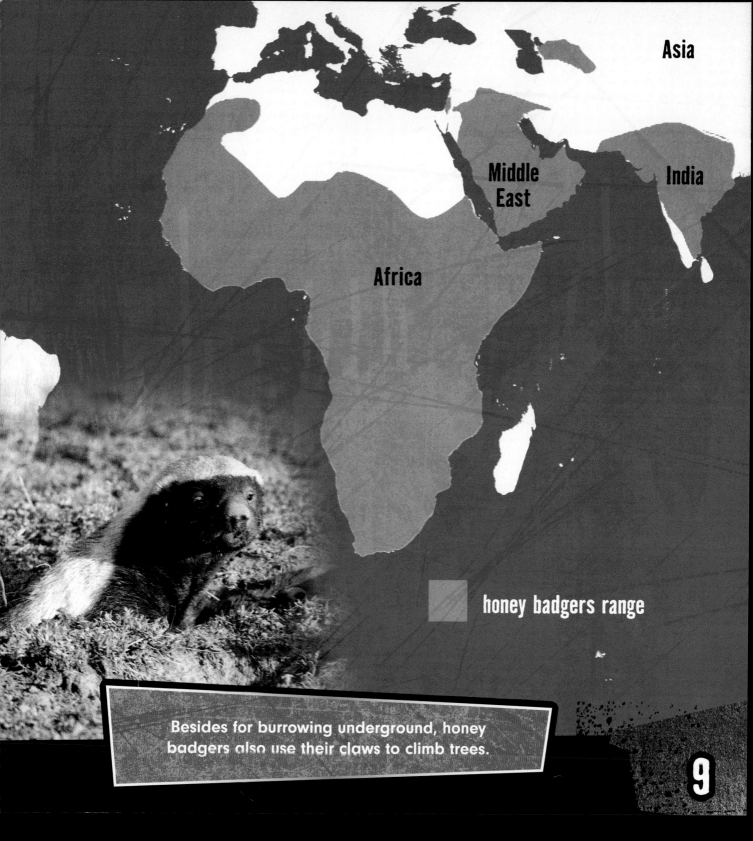

Asia

Middle
East

India

Africa

honey badgers range

Besides for burrowing underground, honey
badgers also use their claws to climb trees.

9

The Hungry Honey Badger

Honey badgers are omnivores. That means they eat both animals and plants. They hunt small **mammals**, birds, **reptiles**, and insects. They sometimes eat plants, including fruit. They also eat carrion, which is another name for animals they come across that are already dead.

Do honey badgers really eat honey? Yes, they do. They also enjoy eating the **larvae** of bees they find in beehives. Scientists think bee stings must not affect honey badgers as much as other animals because they're stung so much while gathering honey.

That's Nasty!

The honey badgers at the San Diego Zoo in California are fed mice and crickets!

You can tell from this honey badger's sharp teeth
that it's a meat eater!

11

No Fear

Many animals run away when they're scared. However, honey badgers attack! It doesn't matter if the animal is much bigger than a honey badger, such as a buffalo, or very dangerous, such as a lion. Honey badgers aren't afraid to take on the scariest of animals.

Honey badgers are known for hunting snakes, even poisonous cobras. They appear to be able to **recover** from a certain amount of cobra venom, or poison. Snakes provide a lot of meat for the honey badger.

That's Nasty!

Honey badgers have been seen trying to attack cars!

These honey badgers are ready to take on a pack of African wild dogs!

Badgers Don't Give Up

What **defenses** do honey badgers have that make them good fighters? First, they have very thick skin. Some animals have a hard time biting through their skin. Even porcupine **quills** may bounce off! Next, their skin is loose. If an animal grabs a honey badger's neck, the honey badger can spin around and bite it! Honey badgers don't have large teeth, but their teeth are very sharp.

Finally, honey badgers will fight for a long time. Other animals just give up or get tired out so the honey badger can get away.

Honey badgers may fight nonstop for more than an hour!

15

Growing Up Badger

Honey badgers mostly like to live alone. However, their hunting territories may overlap. Groups of honey badgers may be seen together if there's a lot of food in one place.

A mother honey badger usually has one baby at a time. She digs a new room, or chamber, in her burrow for the baby. It's born without fur and with its eyes closed. A baby honey badger stays with its mother for up to 2 years. During that time, it learns to hunt from its mother.

A mother honey badger plays with her baby in a zoo.

17

And Stinky, Too!

Honey badgers look a bit like skunks, another member of the weasel family. Like skunks, honey badgers can make things pretty tough for animals' noses.

The honey badger has a body part called a gland at the base of its tail. The gland makes smelly liquid that the honey badger can **release** if it feels like it's in danger. The smell doesn't last as long as a skunk's stink, but it still works! It drives away predators.

That's Nasty!

Honey badgers also use their "stink" to mark their territory and keep other honey badgers away.

skunk

In zoos, honey badgers can live up to 24 years. In the wild, they usually only live about 7 years.

Wild Partners

Honey badgers may be nasty to a lot of animals, but there's at least one animal they get along with. A bird called the greater honey guide may lead the honey badger to beehives. There, the badger rips the hive open and eats what it wants. Then, the bird gets to eat the rest. However, some scientists think it's actually the honey badger that leads the honey guide to the hive.

Honey badgers aren't spotted in the wild very often. There are still many questions left unanswered about these fearsome creatures.

That's Nasty!

Because honey badgers destroy hives, they're sometimes killed by beekeepers.

tough, thick skin

ability to fight for a long time

sharp teeth

Honey Badgers: So Nasty!

are less affected by cobra venom and bee stings

fight animals larger than they are

greater honey guide

Glossary

adaptation: a change in a type of animal that makes it better able to live in its surroundings

burrow: a hole made by an animal in which it lives or hides

defense: a way of guarding against an enemy

habitat: the natural place where an animal or plant lives

larvae: bugs in an early life stage that have a wormlike form. The singular form is "larva."

mammal: a warm-blooded animal that has a backbone and hair, breathes air, and feeds milk to its young

quill: a sharp, stiff point on the body of an animal

recover: to get back to a normal condition

release: to let something out

reptile: an animal covered with scales or plates that breathes air, has a backbone, and lays eggs, such as a turtle, snake, lizard, or crocodile

weasel: a small, meat-eating animal with a long body and tail and short legs

For More Information

Books

Gates, Margo. *Honey Badgers.* Minneapolis, MN: Bellwether Media, 2014.

Quinlan, Julia J. *Honey Badgers.* New York, NY: PowerKids Press, 2013.

Websites

Honey Badger (Mellivora capensis)
www.arkive.org/honey-badger/mellivora-capensis/
Check out many photos of the fearsome honey badger.

Honey Badger (Ratel)
animals.sandiegozoo.org/animals/honey-badger-ratel
Read lots of fun facts about this amazing animal.

Honey Badgers
ngm.nationalgeographic.com/ngm/0409/feature6/fulltext.html
Find out what scientists discovered about honey badgers in the wild.

Publisher's note to educators and parents: Our editors have carefully reviewed these websites to ensure that they are suitable for students. Many websites change frequently, however, and we cannot guarantee that a site's future contents will continue to meet our high standards of quality and educational value. Be advised that students should be closely supervised whenever they access the Internet.

Index